I'm Into You, Jesus.

I'm Into You, Jesus.

Unlocking the door to INTIMACY
and activating the power.

JACKIE AMISSAH–NUNOO

XULON PRESS

Xulon Press
2301 Lucien Way #415
Maitland, FL 32751
407.339.4217
www.xulonpress.com

© 2018 by JACKIE AMISSAH–NUNOO

All rights reserved solely by the author. The author guarantees all contents are original and do not infringe upon the legal rights of any other person or work. No part of this book may be reproduced in any form without the permission of the author. The views expressed in this book are not necessarily those of the publisher.

Unless otherwise indicated, Scripture quotations taken from the Amplified Bible (AMP). Copyright © 1954, 1958, 1962, 1964, 1965, 1987 by The Lockman Foundation. Used by permission. All rights reserved.

Scripture quotations taken from the King James Version (KJV) – *public domain.*

Scripture quotations taken from the New American Standard Bible (NASB). Copyright © 1960, 1962, 1963, 1968, 1971, 1972, 1973, 1975, 1977, 1995 by The Lockman Foundation. Used by permission. All rights reserved.

Scripture quotations taken from the Holy Bible, New International Version (NIV). Copyright © 1973, 1978, 1984, 2011 by Biblica, Inc.™. Used by permission. All rights reserved.

Scripture quotations taken from the New King James Version (NKJV). Copyright © 1982 by Thomas Nelson, Inc. Used by permission. All rights reserved.

Scripture quotations taken from the Holy Bible, New Living Translation (NLT). Copyright ©1996, 2004, 2007 by Tyndale House Foundation. Used by permission of Tyndale House Publishers, Inc.

Printed in the United States of America.

ISBN-13: 978-1-54564-627-4

DEDICATION.

This book is dedicated to my
FLAMINGFIREGIRL team.
Thank you for your endless sacrifices.
Thanks for serving the Lord with me and
for giving yourself to God's work.
I love you each uniquely. Let's serve
God together forever!

CONTENTS

CAN WE BE FRIENDS? ix

1. OBSESSED WITH JESUS AND UNASHAMED 1
2. THE SECRET PLACE – THE PRAYER CLOSET 7
3. YES, LORD, I WILL GO, I WILL DO IT . . . 13
4. I SEE YOU, JESUS 18
5. PRAY WITHOUT CEASING IN EVERY SEASON 22
6. WAIT, I CAN FEEL THE FIRE 29
7. INTIMATE WORSHIPPER 43
8. HOLD TIGHTLY TO THE WORD 48
9. DYING TO SELF 52
10. GOD, DO YOU TRUST ME? 56
11. TO LIVE IS CHRIST, TO DIE IS GAIN. . . . 59
12. THE SECRET. 64

CAN WE BE FRIENDS?

Hi There! I am so excited to spend some quality time with you. I'll tell you a little bit about myself. My name is Jackie and to tell you the truth, I'm not exactly a reader but I can TALK for the whole world. I love God so much and honestly this love burns in my heart and bones like a fire and I just can't contain it. God deeply desires an intimate relationship with you and He told me to write this book to push you into the prayer closet! Yup, you!

So as you embark on this reading journey, it's my prayer that you prayerfully read these chapters and I pray that it stirs up and reignites the fire of God in your heart. I pray that this fire so consumes you that you feel it in your very bones! When this happens, you actually can't shut up and keep Jesus to yourself! You would rather preach the truth of God's WORD than stay silent and watch people lust or party their way to Hell.

So, in this book I'm going to be talking about intimacy with Jesus and why it's a big deal. The amazing part is there are some secrets that can only be unlocked through your intimacy with Jesus. If you already love Jesus or you want to love Jesus, then this is the right book for you. Also, if you love secrets, then you definitely picked up the right book!

Finally, if you're like me and you don't exactly like reading, I am praying for a good attention span for you because you've gotta read this one!

May you tangibly feel God's presence and may He anoint you with His fire as you read this book!

CHAPTER 1

OBSSESED WITH JESUS & unashamed.

> "Jesus replied, "'You must love the Lord your God with all your heart, all your soul, and all your mind."
> Matthew 22:37 NLT

> "Love is not only something you feel; it is something you do."
> – David Wilkerson.

> "Jesus Christ knows the worst about you. Nonetheless, He is the one who loves you the most." – A. W. Tozer

With all that's going on around us in this world, I don't think I'm the only one who thinks there has to be more to life. We need to fix our gaze on something solid, something everlasting and something that never fades away. No matter the number of years you've lived on this earth, I'm pretty sure you can attest to the fact that Isaiah 40:8 is flawless.

WE NEED TO FIX OUR GAZE ON SOMETHING SOLID, SOMETHING EVERLASTING AND SOMETHING THAT NEVER FADES AWAY.

"The grass withers and the flowers fade, but the word of our God stands forever.'" Isaiah 40:8 NLT

Seasons change, people change, people leave, people disappoint and people die but one thing is for sure, God's WORD is forever. According to John 1:1, we understand that the WORD is GOD. He cannot be described with one word. Even if you put every single word that has ever existed together, it still wouldn't be enough to describe our Great God. He is THE WORD that was manifested in flesh.

"And the Word became flesh and dwelt among us, and we beheld His glory, the glory as of the only begotten of the Father, full of grace and truth."

John 1:14 NKJV

With sin on the high, we need a safe place. In this our world where sin is the "new trend," we desperately need a strong tower or maybe a solid rock to hold on to. Otherwise, we will be swept away by the sweet smelling attractiveness of sin into the deep, dark sea of destruction. Yes, we need a ROCK. We need a STRONG TOWER. We need a PERMANENT FLOAT to cling tightly to in the hopes of someday reaching that Safe Solid Rock. This is no exaggeration; this is the sad reality.

IN THIS OUR WORLD WHERE SIN IS THE "NEW TREND," WE DESPERATELY NEED A STRONG TOWER

Well, it is not a hopeless situation. Should 'hopeless' even be a word when Jesus is alive? It can never be so! With Jesus, we have HOPE. You know why? Because He doesn't just give us HOPE, He is our HOPE. Once you give Him your whole heart and purpose to love Him with the entirety of your being, HOPE is all yours. The amazing part is, with JESUS our HOPES become reality. Of course, once your hopes align with HIS WORD.

Yes, there is sin and evil all over us. Temptation is on the High. You don't need a supernatural encounter to know that the devil is working extremely hard; he knows his time is up!

The good news is, although the waves of this sweet smelling sea of sin seem so strong, we have a solid rock that we can climb on to. We have a strong tower that we can run into. We have a safe hiding place. That's Jesus! Oh yes, you might already find yourself swimming in the deep end of this sea of sin but your lifeguard, Jesus, walks on water. He is calling out to you. He is stretching out His hands to you. "Are my hands short that it cannot save?" The Lord keeps asking you, but you can't hear HIM because you are distracted.

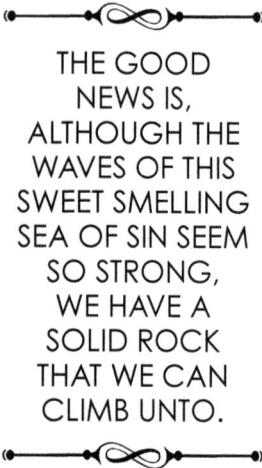

THE GOOD NEWS IS, ALTHOUGH THE WAVES OF THIS SWEET SMELLING SEA OF SIN SEEM SO STRONG, WE HAVE A SOLID ROCK THAT WE CAN CLIMB UNTO.

"Behold, the Lord's hand is not shortened, that it cannot save…"   Isaiah 59:1 NKJV

Jesus is the answer. Jesus is the love you've been searching for. Jesus is the love story you've been daydreaming about. He is your hero. His love for you is so deep; it's unending. In fact, He didn't just buy you gifts to win your love, He gave you the greatest gift

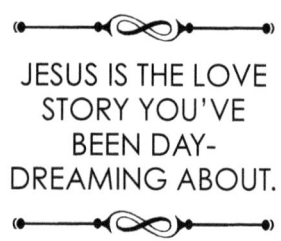

JESUS IS THE LOVE STORY YOU'VE BEEN DAYDREAMING ABOUT.

– His life, His blood. He thought you were worth dying for. He thought it right to give it all up for you. This MAN thought His reputation was worth giving up–for you. He thought leaving His throne, casting down His crown and dying a criminal's death on a cross was so worth it just for you. JUST for you.

Doesn't He deserve your love? Doesn't He deserve your heart? Doesn't He deserve your full attention? Doesn't He deserve your service? Doesn't He deserve constant sacrifice from you? Doesn't He deserve it all? Doesn't He deserve your life? I must say that falling in love with Jesus is the best decision I have ever made. Deciding to push my obsession to Jesus and deciding to fix my gaze on Him was the best decision ever. You have absolutely nothing to lose and even if you've lost something, your restoration is in Him. Jesus is your hero. I'm so obsessed with Jesus and I'm unashamed, shouldn't you also be? What are you waiting for? What's your excuse?

I'M INTO YOU, JESUS.

> **JESUS,** I'm obsessed with you.

CHAPTER 2

THE SECRET PLACE – THE PRAYER CLOSET.

"He who dwells in the secret place of the Most High Shall abide under the shadow of the Almighty."
Psalms 91:1 NKJV

"Inside the Tent of Meeting, the Lord would speak to Moses face to face, as one speaks to a friend."
Exodus 33:11 NLT

"The closet means simply to be shut in with God anywhere, at any time giving God quality chosen time."
– David Wilkerson

> "A sinning man will stop praying and a praying man will stop sinning."
> –Leonard Ravenhill

I never knew love could be so tangible. I never knew love could be so deep. I never knew love could be unending. I never knew love could be so beautiful. I never knew love could be perfect–till I met Him and then I realized that love was a person. Wait! Hold on, are you saying that love is a person that I can know? YES! Love is THE person that you should know– INTIMATELY.

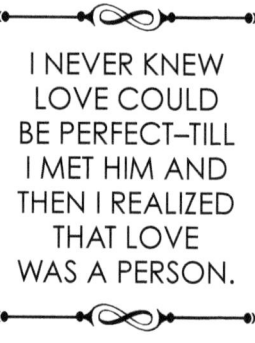

I NEVER KNEW LOVE COULD BE PERFECT–TILL I MET HIM AND THEN I REALIZED THAT LOVE WAS A PERSON.

How can you know love intimately and live in depression and isolation? Should that not be an abomination? You can actually know LOVE deeply but you choose to live in fear and anxiety. I find that quite baffling. Perfect love casts out fear, rememember?

God is love and you can know God intimately! How awesome is that? You make time for things you love, don't you? You create space for people you love, don't you? You make sacrifices for people you love, don't you?

I always claimed to love the Lord but one day my love for God was challenged. The Holy Spirit whispered to me, "you say you love God but you have 24 hours in a day, how many do you give back to Him? How many do you spend with Him? 20minutes? 30minutes? Is that love? Are you sure you have a relationship with God?" That was a hard pill for me to swallow. I can talk to people I admire and love for hours but how is it that when it comes to God, we think it's okay to spend only 10minutes with Him? I don't know about you, but I can't date someone who barely spends an hour with me daily whether on facetime, skype or in person. A sister needs some attention sir. Jokes! (not really, I'm actually serious)

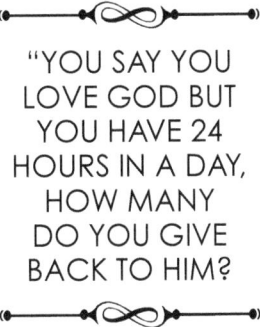

"YOU SAY YOU LOVE GOD BUT YOU HAVE 24 HOURS IN A DAY, HOW MANY DO YOU GIVE BACK TO HIM?

Ever since that confrontation from the Holy Spirit, I knew that God deserved more from me. No wonder the scriptures say, "They honor me with their lips yet their hearts are so far from me!" Matthew 15:8. When we read such scriptures, we think about friends we believe are living deeply sinful lives but we forget to look at the person reading this book. Ouch!

But, how can you sing songs like this:

"To worship you I live, to worship you I live, I live to worship you."

and

"Lord, I give you my heart, I give you my soul, I live for you alone, every breath that I take, every moment, I'm awake, Lord have your way in me." with actions that scream the exact opposite?

How can you sing songs like these and spend only 30 minutes out of 24 hours with God daily? Do we think God is a fool? How can you tell Him, "...Every breath that I take, every moment I'm awake, Lord have your way in me," and live prayerless lives? Let me tell you this now, God is not mocked!

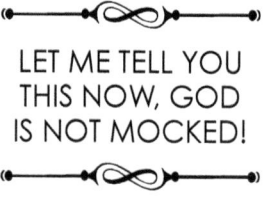

LET ME TELL YOU THIS NOW, GOD IS NOT MOCKED!

Run into the secret closet. Make time for God. Spend quality time with God! PRAY, PRAY, PRAY! Personally, I like to plan out my day and intentionally slot in hours for prayer and time with God in HIS Presence. It is the most important thing on my daily to-do list and I treat it as such. How intentional are you with your prayer life? How serious are you about your quiet time with the Lord?

Why do you think David desperately said, "Cast me not away from your Presence, please don't take your Spirit from me?" Living a prayerless life in these end-times is a death-trap. You are basically walking dead. The Spirit gives life therefore without the Holy Spirit, you are dead within.

"It is the Spirit who gives life; the flesh profits nothing. The words that I speak to you are spirit, and they are life." John 6:63 NKJV

You need to rise up in prayer! You need God! You need His Spirit! You need power in these last days to combat fear and timidity. You also need power to withstand temptation. This power is only made available through the Holy Spirit and the Holy Spirit only comes upon a person who prays. You need to pray! You need to spend hours in prayer. If you're going to serve the Lord or be a minister of the Gospel, what exactly are you trying to do by spending only 30minutes in prayer daily? Lives are connected to your prayer life! Your family's breakthrough is in your prayer life! Your freedom from bondages and addiction is in your prayer life! Your blessing is in your prayer life! As long as you have breath in you, PRAY!

There's something about setting the atmosphere in your prayer closet that allows you to stay in there for hours. Since I'm in college, my prayer closet is my apartment room. I named and labelled my room, BETHEL and I told God that I wanted His presence to be extremely tangible in my room. I also told Him that I wanted to encounter Him like never before and I desired an encounter just like Jacob had when he named the place Bethel. (Genesis 28:17-19). I dedicated the room to God and I told him to have His way in there. Ever since then, I cannot count the number of encounters I have had in there. I can stay in my room all day just loving on my sweet Jesus. This can be your story too; you just have to make sure you set the atmosphere in your prayer closet for an encounter with God.

Get into that prayer closet now!

CHAPTER 3

YES, LORD, I WILL GO, I WILL DO IT.

"Also I heard the voice of the Lord, saying: "Whom shall I send, And who will go for Us?" Then I said, "Here am I! Send me.""

Isaiah 6:8 NKJV

"When I said yes, God did more than I could ask for." – Wynter Pitts

Giving God my YES was the wisest decision I ever made. Our understanding is flawed when we think we are doing God a favor by saying YES to Him or Choosing OBEDIENCE. No, my darling, you're doing your beautiful self a lovely favor. You need God more than you'll ever know.

I clearly remember that morning during my quiet time when God instructed me to start the FLAMINGFIREGIRL Ministry. With tears in my eyes, pain in my heart and unanswered prayers (or so I thought), I said YES. God gave me the scripture Hebrews 1:7, "In Speaking of the angels, he says, he makes his angels spirits and his servants as FLAMES OF FIRE." The Lord told me, "I'm sick and tired of Luke warmness, start an Instagram page and do what I tell you to do going forward." I said, "YES."

To tell you the truth, it was one of the toughest seasons of my life. I felt like everything was falling apart, I felt broken and crushed and in all honestly, I felt like God had disappointed me. I felt defeated, useless, daft, not worthy enough to work for God, the list goes on. Somehow, I overlooked all of this and said YES to God although, in that season, there wasn't a day that went by that I did not cry or weep. But, there was one thing I knew for sure, that I was NEVER letting Jesus go neither was I going to let His fire in me go out!

When I say, I would've never in my life imagined that a book could come out of me, I mean it. For years, I have been battling with DEEP doubt in my intelligence. So, I had no idea what God was trying to do but I trusted His plan for my life above my problems. Often times, we trust in the success story of our problems over the good and unchangeable plans God has for us.

> OFTEN TIMES, WE TRUST IN THE SUCCESS STORY OF OUR PROBLEMS OVER THE GOOD AND UNCHANGEABLE PLANS GOD HAS FOR US.

Your YES counts. Someone somewhere is counting on your "YES." Generations unborn are relying on you to step out on OBEDIENCE.

Please understand that your YES to God, is a NO to the world. You can't carry out your God-given purpose if you're living a lukewarm life. It just can't work. Giving God your YES is a permanent decision to go ALL out for His Kingdom and its righteousness and NOTHING LESS.

Your obedience to God in your darkest seasons holds SO much power. More than you can imagine.

Joseph remained obedient to God in the pit and in the prison and He became the highest in command in Egypt.

Abraham remained obedient to God when His situation should have led him otherwise. He became the Father of many nations. Today, you exist because Abraham remained obedient in Faith. You are a descendant of Abraham.

Jesus was obedient to the point of death on a cross and because of that, today, at the mention of His name, everything in Heaven, on earth and under the earth trembles to their knees. JUST at the mention of HIS name – JESUS!

Your obedience truly counts. No matter what you're currently walking through, God still has a purpose for you, He still has an assignment for you. Ask God to reveal to you what assignment He has for you. It pays to take your eyes off yourself and focus on reaching out to someone who desperately needs Jesus. Don't let your problems blind you to the millions of souls in the valley of the shadow of death who need the Jesus that you have!

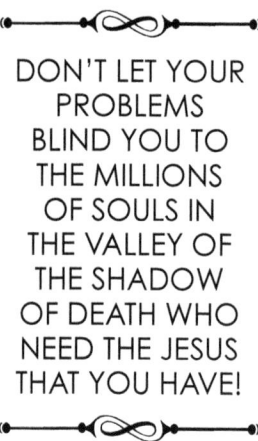

DON'T LET YOUR PROBLEMS BLIND YOU TO THE MILLIONS OF SOULS IN THE VALLEY OF THE SHADOW OF DEATH WHO NEED THE JESUS THAT YOU HAVE!

Giving God your YES doesn't mean you won't go through the fire. Rather, it gives you the assurance of going through the fire and coming out stronger and unharmed because God will always be with you. Always. He will be with you in the furnace, in the den of lions, in the wilderness and on the battlefield.

Give God your "YES" today! That's all that really matters.

CHAPTER 4

I SEE YOU, JESUS!

"In all your ways acknowledge Him,
And He shall direct your paths."
                    Proverbs 3:6 NKJV

"If God gives you a few more years, remember, it is not yours. Your time must honor God, your activity must honor God, and everything you do must honor God."   – A. W. Tozer

The Bible is as clear as it can get. Acknowledge the Lord in all your ways and HE will direct your path. Basically, don't just tell Jesus you're into Him, let your actions show! You acknowledge the presence of a chairman of an event not just by mentioning His name or merely introducing Him but you accompany this introduction by giving Him a seat at the High table. As if that wasn't enough, we spice all of that up by giving him quality treatment. Often times, the attendees of such programs receive nothing as the chairman is professionally served some fancy goodies.

How is it that we acknowledge the presence of reputable men on earth and fail to acknowledge God? Men who are here one minute and are gone the other. Men who only have power because God chose to give it to them. Men who are only alive because of the breath of God in them!

MEN WHO ONLY HAVE POWER BECAUSE GOD CHOSE TO GIVE IT TO THEM.

Too often, you start off our day by telling God to be with you, and then throughout the day you talk to everyone but Him, engage everyone and everything but Him. How dare you? How dare you fail to acknowledge the presence of the almighty God in your life? As if it wasn't enough that you ignored Him, you engaged in activities and did things that grieved His Spirit! Forgetting that you are sternly warned not to grieve the Holy Spirit. (Ephesians 4:30) Oh, how often we displease God! Talk of the mercy of God!

Recently, the Holy Spirit gave me a powerful revelation in this scripture,

"You believe that there is one God, good! Even the demons believe it and shudder."   James 2:19

It was this – IF even the demons shudder at the thought of the God we serve and we, Christians feel absolutely nothing at the thought and mention of His name, are we any better than the demons?

We talk about how demons disgust us and we constantly express our hatred for demons, yet the irony of this is that, even these nasty demons, tremble at the mention of the name Jesus. Isn't it a shame that those of us who claim to be Christ-like, are rather unmoved and unrepentant at the mention of THIS name?

Yes, the Bible is comparing human beings to demons because really, we seem to have lost the fear of God in our hearts!

Don't let this be you, be that one person who acknowledges the Lord in all you do. It doesn't matter what people have to say about it.

Personally, I make a very conscious effort to acknowledge God in all I do. This means intentionally seeking to find God in everything. Even in seemingly "normal" moments, I look for God because God is always in the detail.

Your very life should be acknowledging to God! Every breath you take and every move you make should be to the glory of God. People must see you and see the Jesus in you. People must encounter you and leave changed because of the Spirit of God within you. You were created to make an impact in this world. The scripture says to acknowledge the Lord and He will direct your path. Once your steps are ordered by God, you can be sure that no matter the mountains you climb and valleys you walk through, you will come out victorious. Once Jesus is in your boat, you can never drown.

To acknowledge God is to recognize His presence and to respect it enough to talk, walk and live as though Jesus were standing right next to you. When you acknowledge God, you do the things that please Him wholeheartedly. Acknowledge JESUS daily in ALL you do, with confidence in your heart; knowing that the HE is with you.

CHAPTER 5

PRAY WITHOUT CEASING IN EVERY SEASON.

"And he spake a parable unto them to this end, that men ought always to pray, and not to faint;"

Luke 18:1 KJV

"Your deliverance is in your unceasing prayer" – Very Rev. Dr. Lawrence Ackah – Miezah (My spiritual father)

Let prayer be your lifestyle. Aside having a prayer closet where you spend quality time with your Lord and personal savior, prayer should be your daily language. Prayer should be your breakfast, lunch, snack, dinner, midnight

> PRAYER SHOULD BE YOUR BREAKFAST, LUNCH, SNACK, DINNER, MIDNIGHT SNACK AND CHEAT MEAL.

Pray Without Ceasing In Every Season.

snack and cheat meal. Pray always. Pray everywhere and anywhere. Pray, pray, pray so your spirit man can be active and strong. Pray so that you do not fall into temptation.

When you're sad, pray.
When you're disappointed pray.
When you're moody, pray.
When you're angry, pray.
When you feel like giving up, pray.
When life knocks you down to your knees, pray.
When it feels like everything is falling apart, pray.
When your heart is broken, pray.
When your spirit is crushed, pray.

When you're happy, pray.
When you're confused, pray.
When life is good, pray.
When you hear bad news, pray.
When you hear good news, pray.
And when life gets so overwhelmingly busy, take a pause, slip away and pray.

"And Jesus often slipped away to other places to be alone so that He could pray." Luke 5:16 ICB

"AND JESUS OFTEN SLIPPED AWAY TO OTHER PLACES TO BE ALONE SO THAT HE COULD PRAY." LUKE 5:16 ICB

I love that Jesus would slip away into isolation to pray! Sometimes, life gets stressful, tiring, demanding and absolutely draining. But, you need to understand that your rest is in God and God alone. Your ability to stay at rest is in your prayer life. No amount of sleep can ever make you feel well rested. I'm sure people always wondered how Jesus had the strength to constantly go about preaching, healing the sick and setting the captives free. This was Jesus' little secret – He would slip away into the wilderness to pray! Prayer recharges you and replenishes your strength. Prayer is powerful and you need to be praying always!

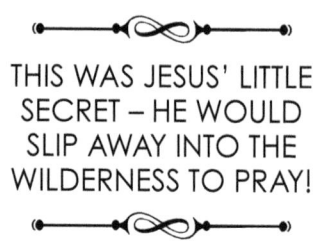

THIS WAS JESUS' LITTLE SECRET – HE WOULD SLIP AWAY INTO THE WILDERNESS TO PRAY!

There is something about praying in the wilderness! Throughout the Bible we see that trend of men of God praying in the wilderness and oh, how the Heavens were opened unto them! When you find yourself in the wilderness, that's not the place to give up HOPE! That's your opportunity to encounter God like never before. Why did Jesus slip away into the wilderness just to pray? For some of us, the Spirit of God will have to push us into the wilderness to humble us and to get us back on our knees in prayer! The wilderness experience is to stir you up in prayer! Don't waste your wilderness experience! Yes, it's not where you wish to be but it's exactly where you need to be to come into contact with God! As you behold Him, you are changed into His image of glory – from one level of glory to a higher level of glory. As you encounter God in the wilderness, you are freed from bondages! The wilderness experience is meant to refine you; it's meant to realign you into your destiny! I'll say this again, the wilderness is not the place to give up, it's your opportunity to become a woman of prayer!

Prayer is the major key. Prayer is where your power lies. You are more active when you are prayerful and you're a stronger when you are prayerful.

Sometimes, we don't understand how we keep making the same mistakes and falling into the same old traps but, if you only pray for 2 minutes when you wake up, pray for 30seconds before eating breakfast, lunch and supper and top it off with another 2-minute prayer before you go to bed at night, what do you expect, my love?

Your spirit is practically malnourished and weak – close to death.

As a believer, prayer is your secret weapon. That's why you can't be a believer and not believe in speaking in tongues. I think it's safe to even call that a sin! You need to know how to pray in the Spirit! Believers everywhere should speak in tongues, that is one sure sign of the Holy Spirit in a person's life!

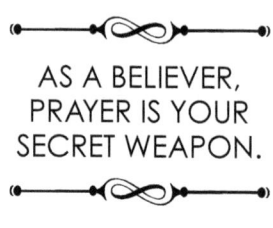
AS A BELIEVER, PRAYER IS YOUR SECRET WEAPON.

You think I'm lying? Ask Peter or read the book of Acts. Speaking in tongues is vital for every Christian! Sometimes, you don't know what to pray about but the Holy Spirit will intercede on your behalf in groanings that cannot be interpreted!

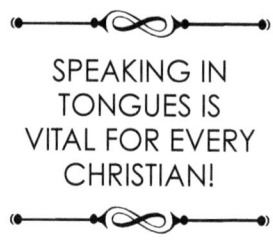
SPEAKING IN TONGUES IS VITAL FOR EVERY CHRISTIAN!

"Likewise the Spirit also helps in our weaknesses. For we do not know what we should pray for as we ought, but the Spirit Himself makes intercession for us with groanings which cannot be uttered."

Romans 8:26 NKJV

If you don't speak in tongues, please ask your Pastor or Spiritual father or anyone you know is maturing in the Faith to pray with you! A believer who doesn't speak in tongues, is like an airplane without wings. It's supposed to fly but it can't and it lacks a vital part. Not to say that praying in the language you speak and understand lacks power. I mean the plane can still move without the wings, it still has tires but it can't soar without its wings.

A BELIEVER WHO DOESN'T SPEAK IN TONGUES, IS LIKE AN AIRPLANE WITHOUT WINGS.

Speaking in tongues takes you to higher heights in the Spirit. Speaking in tongues charges your inner man, quickens your mortal body and edifies you. Pray without ceasing in every season.

Prayer is a necessity. As the deer pants for the waters, so should your spirit long to be in prayer. Make huge sacrifices to ensure you become a woman of prayer. Don't be afraid to take a day off, lock yourself up in your room and seek the face of Jesus! Your power lies in who you interact with. Whilst people take pride in their interaction with Heads of State and millionaires, as a child of God, your pride should be in your constant interaction with the Most High – the One who gives life. The King of All Kings, The ONE who spoke this world into being and THE ONE whom, at the thought of His power, all of hell trembles! This God is your God and it is an absolute privilege that you can freely and boldly come to Him in prayer. Pray in everything and about everything; BE A WOMAN OF PRAYER. Therein lies your power as a believer!

This should be you from today, "Can't stop, won't stop praying!" Pray always and don't you ever get tired!

CHAPTER 6

WAIT, I CAN FEEL THE FIRE!

"Then I said, "I will not make mention of Him, Nor speak anymore in His name." But His word was in my heart like a burning fire Shut up in my bones; I was weary of holding it back, And I could not."
Jeremiah 20:9 NKJV

"But if I say I'll never mention the Lord or speak in his name, his word burns in my heart like a fire. It's like a fire in my bones! I am worn out trying to hold it in! I can't do it!"
Jeremiah 20:9 NLT

Oh my! I think I can feel something in my body, I can feel it in my heart. Wait, it's spreading–my bones, I can feel something in my bones! It's burning, I think it's fire. This fire feels different, it must be from God, the consuming fire!

Is it just me or this is the season to be set on fire for the Lord? Now is the time, today is the day to allow the consuming fire to consume you with His fire!

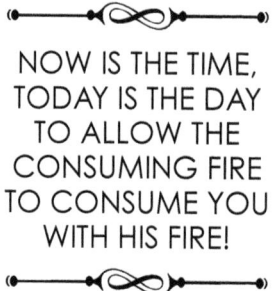

NOW IS THE TIME, TODAY IS THE DAY TO ALLOW THE CONSUMING FIRE TO CONSUME YOU WITH HIS FIRE!

You've played around for too long, you've been distracted for far too long. It's about time!

If you're still holding on to Luke warmness after reading this Chapter, please put this book down!

You see, being set on fire is one of the major benefits you gain from getting intimate with the Lord. You cannot come in contact with the consuming fire and be lukewarm. That's a problem!

YOU CANNOT COME IN CONTACT WITH THE CONSUMING FIRE AND BE LUKEWARM.

The God you serve is a God of fire and you CANNOT encounter Him and remain the same. This fire consumes and I'm about to show you what I mean by this.

THE GOD OF FIRE.

I'm going to break this down for you and by the time I'm done, give me a reason why you won't be on fire for the Lord. First of all, this message isn't for a select few. It's for everyone. Anyone with EARS must HEAR this!

""Anyone with ears to hear must listen to the Spirit and understand what he is saying to the churches." Revelation 2:29 NLT

QUALITIES of the God of FIRE.

THRONE OF FIRE.

""As I looked, thrones were put in their places. And God, the Eternal One, sat on his throne. His clothes were white like snow. And the hair on His head was white like wool. His throne was made from fire. And the wheels of His throne were blazing with fire." Daniel 7:9 ICB

The very throne of God is made from fire!

"PILLARS OF FIRE"

"Then I saw another mighty angel coming down from heaven, surrounded by a cloud, with a rainbow over his head. His face shone like the sun, and his feet were like pillars of fire."

Revelation 10:1 NLT

If just the legs of angels are like pillars of fire, you, the human being created in the very image of THE CONSUMING FIRE should be entirely ablaze for God. It should not just be your hands, your legs, your eyes or your lips. Your whole being is supposed to be a flame of fire.

This is who God created you to be, FIRE. Fire consumes, Fire spreads and fire burns. You cannot be consumed by fire while holding on to certain sins. This fire should burn away chaff from your life. You should be so consumed by the fire of God that whoever comes into contact with you MUST catch the fire! If what is burning within your heart and bones is truly fire, it must consume you, it must spread to others and it must burn away chaff!

THIS IS WHO GOD CREATED YOU TO BE, FIRE.

The sad truth is that, when you're not on fire for God, you're not living up to God's standard for you. You're actually living outside the will of God and that's DANGEROUS because you're safest in God's will.

THE GOD WITH EYES LIKE FIRE.

"His head and his hair were white like wool, as white as snow. And his eyes were like flames of fire."   Revelation 1:14 NLT

Can you be intimate with GOD without catching this fire? The Bible says that Moses knew God face to face. Moses was the man who was called out from the fire! No wonder he did marvelous works. When you are consumed by the fire of God, you can't be idle and your life cannot be meaningless. The fire of God within you will push you out of your comfort zone to WORK for God.

Throughout the Bible, I don't think there was anyone who gave God excuses more than Moses did.

Take a look at this: (Exodus 3:9-14, 4:1-13)

"Look! The cry of the people of Israel has reached me, and I have seen how harshly the Egyptians abuse them. Now go, for I am sending you to Pharaoh. You must lead my people Israel out of Egypt."

EXCUSE 1: But Moses protested to God, "Who am I to appear before Pharaoh? Who am I to lead the people of Israel out of Egypt?"

God answered, "I will be with you. And this is your sign that I am the one who has sent you: When you have brought the people out of Egypt, you will worship God at this very mountain." But Moses protested,

EXCUSE 2: "If I go to the people of Israel and tell them, 'The God of your ancestors has sent me to you,' they will ask me, 'What is his name?' Then what should I tell them?"

God replied to Moses, "I Am Who I Am. Say this to the people of Israel: I Am has sent me to you."

EXCUSE 3: "But Moses protested again, "What if they won't believe me or listen to me? What if they say, 'The Lord never appeared to you'?"'

"Then the Lord asked him, "What is that in your hand?" "A shepherd's staff," Moses replied. "Throw it down on the ground," the Lord told him. So Moses threw down the staff, and it turned into a snake! Moses jumped back. Then the Lord told him, "Reach out and grab its tail." So Moses reached out and grabbed it, and it turned back into a shepherd's staff in his hand. "Perform this sign," the Lord told him. "Then they will believe that the Lord, the God of their ancestors—the God of Abraham, the God of Isaac, and the God of Jacob—really has appeared to you."'

EXCUSE 4: "But Moses pleaded with the Lord, "O Lord, I'm not very good with words. I never have been, and I'm not now, even though you have spoken to me. I get tongue-tied, and my words get tangled."'

"Then the Lord asked Moses, "Who makes a person's mouth? Who decides whether people speak or do not speak, hear or do not hear, see or do not see? Is it not I, the Lord? Now go! I will be with you as you speak, and I will instruct you in what to say."'

EXCUSE 5: 'But Moses again pleaded, "Lord, please! Send anyone else."'

You need more than just love and excitement for the things of God to do and to be who God has called you to be. You can love God and you can be excited about serving HIM but you need the fire to get out of your comfort zone to do exploits and to do the dirty work. You need the fire of God to speak the truth of God's WORD with boldness.

YOU NEED MORE THAN JUST LOVE AND EXCITEMENT FOR THE THINGS OF GOD TO DO AND TO BE WHO GOD HAS CALLED YOU TO BE.

God is looking for people who will stand up and stand out for His Kingdom. He is looking for "Pauls" and "Stephens" of our day.

We need to say good-bye to shyness and timidity. What is timidity to a person on fire for the Lord?

You see, the truth is, we all have reasons why we do not consider ourselves qualified for God's work just like Moses did. But, there is something about being called by the consuming fire! There is just something about the Baptism of the Holy Spirit and fire!

John the Baptist, told the people, "I baptize you with water but one is coming who is greater than I am. He will baptize you with the Holy Spirit and with FIRE. (Matthew 3:11)

You NEED the fire of God! John was talking about Jesus Christ. Jesus is the one who baptizes us with fire. You can never access this fire if you're not intimate with Jesus and you cannot be intimate with

> YOU CAN NEVER ACCESS THIS FIRE IF YOU'RE NOT INTIMATE WITH JESUS AND YOU CANNOT BE INTIMATE WITH JESUS WITHOUT RECEIVING THE BAPTISM OF THE HOLY SPIRIT AND FIRE!

Jesus without receiving the baptism of the Holy Spirit and fire!

THE GOD WHOSE WORDS ARE FIRE.

"But if I say I'll never mention the Lord or speak in his name, his word burns in my heart like a fire. It's like a fire in my bones! I am worn out trying to hold it in! I can't do it!" Jeremiah 20:9 NLT

If the very words of God are fire, there's absolutely no way you can communicate with God daily without being consumed by the fire of His Word! You can't be reading the same Holy Bible I read daily and walk out of your prayer closet unchanged, unless, it's not the Holy Bible!

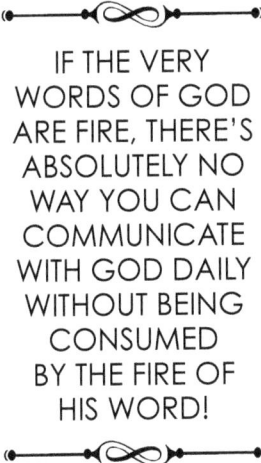

IF THE VERY WORDS OF GOD ARE FIRE, THERE'S ABSOLUTELY NO WAY YOU CAN COMMUNICATE WITH GOD DAILY WITHOUT BEING CONSUMED BY THE FIRE OF HIS WORD!

If this pertains to you, then you've been doing something wrong. You cannot claim to have a relationship with the Lord and be a lukewarm Christian! It's absolutely impossible! God is calling you to a deeper place in Him. Enough with the shallow Christianity, throw it away! It's yielding no fruits. Above all, It's not enhancing the Kingdom of God. What's the point of your Christianity if it's yielding no fruit?

THE GOD WHO CALLS BY FIRE.

"There the angel of the Lord appeared to him in a blazing fire from the middle of a bush. Moses stared in amazement. Though the bush was engulfed in flames, it didn't burn up. "This is amazing," Moses said to himself. "Why isn't that bush burning up? I must go see it." When the Lord saw Moses coming to take a closer look, God called to him from the middle of the bush, "Moses! Moses!" "Here I am!" Moses replied. "Do not come any closer," the Lord warned. "Take off your sandals, for you are standing on holy ground. I am the God of your father —the God of Abraham, the God of Isaac, and the God of Jacob." When Moses heard this, he covered his face because he was afraid to look at God."

Exodus 3:2-6 NLT

When the God of fire calls you to Himself like He's doing now, you need to INTENTIONALLY drop some things off. Moses had to take off his sandals! You must reverence and fear God enough to let go of certain habits and people.

For some of you, this may be certain relationships, boys, ungodly music, etc.

For me, I had to drop a relationship, worldly music and other little distractions. I took them off and responded to the voice that called out to me from the fire!

Of course, there are some cases where people are addicted to certain behaviors, things or people and in those cases, they need to be delivered either by an anointed man of God or by personal fervent prayer and fasting. However, there are some habits and people that we just don't want to let go off. These are hindrances we can easily take off but we choose not to. Whatever yours may be, take it off and RUN, a voice is calling out to you from the FIRE.

You know when you're watching a movie at home and someone from another room is trying to tell you something? The amazing part is that most of the time no matter how soft the voice is, you'll hear your name but with the instruction that follows, you just might have to turn the volume down to hear effectively when the instruction follows.

You might have heard a call, or a strong impression of a call from God. You might feel like your name was mentioned but if you don't take that extra step to turn the volume of this world all the way down, you'll miss out on the instruction and specific assignment that God has for you.

THE GOD WHO ANSWERS BY FIRE.

"Then you call on the name of your gods, and I will call on the name of the LORD; and the God who answers by fire, He is God." So all the people answered and said, "It is well spoken.""

I Kings 18:24 NKJV

"David built an altar there to the Lord and sacrificed burnt offerings and peace offerings. And when David prayed, the Lord answered him by sending fire from heaven to burn up the offering on the altar."

1 Chronicles 21:26 NLT

Choose the God of fire today. Allow Him to consume you with His fire. It's either you experience the fire of God now and you allow the consuming fire to set you on fire now or you experience hell-fire later.

BECAUSE, THE HARSH TRUTH IS THIS: NO LUKEWARM SOUL WILL ENTER THE KINGDOM OF HEAVEN!

Because, the harsh Truth is this: No Lukewarm soul will enter the Kingdom of Heaven!

So, how do you keep this fire burning? How do you prevent this fire from never quenching? Stay in the secret place of God. You keep the fire burning by getting out of your comfort zone to spread the gospel. Get out of your room; get out of your house and share your story with someone. Tell someone about Jesus, encourage them in the Lord. So many people are hurting out there and they need the Jesus that you have.

You also need to be very conscious and intentional about what you feed your spirit with.

"Guard your heart above all else, for it determines the course of your life." Proverbs 4:23 NLT

Filter out unnecessary things from your life: Friends, worldly celebrities, worldly music (it has ABSOLUTELY NO BENEFIT in your SPIRITUAL LIFE), and the like. Ask the Holy Spirit for wisdom to know what to filter out and ask for strength to let go of the things that will be difficult to filter out of your life!

FINALLY, LET THE HOLY SPIRIT BE YOUR BESTFRIEND.

Constantly talk to the Holy Spirit throughout your day. Let the Holy Spirit teach and explain things to you, from the WORD through to common things you'd need to understand more deeply in this life.

""There is so much more I want to tell you, but you can't bear it now. When the Spirit of truth comes, he will guide you into all truth. He will not speak on his own but will tell you what he has heard. He will tell you about the future. He will bring me glory by telling you whatever he receives from me." John 16:12-14 NLT

The Holy Spirit should be your number one go-to person In life!

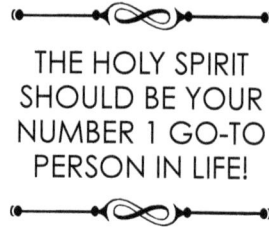

THE HOLY SPIRIT SHOULD BE YOUR NUMBER 1 GO-TO PERSON IN LIFE!

CHAPTER 7

INTIMATE WORSHIPPER

"But the time is coming—indeed it's here now—when true worshipers will worship the Father in spirit and in truth. The Father is looking for those who will worship him that way."
John 4:23 NLT

"Her sister, Mary, sat at the Lord's feet, listening to what he taught."
Luke 10:39

"We must never rest until everything inside us worships God"
– A. W Tozer

I will boldly and gladly admit that my worship got me to this point. Worship is extremely powerful and it is the one thing that gets to God faster and more directly than prayer. Aside that, who doesn't like some good, Spirit-filled music?

And yes, worship is more than just music, it's a lifestyle but for this chapter, I would like to focus on the music aspect of worship.

Many of the encounters and visions I've had have been during my intimate worship sessions with God. Sometimes in Church but mostly when I'm in my secret closet spending quality time with my Sweet Jesus. Worship is deep, extremely deep and it is intimate beyond the description of words.

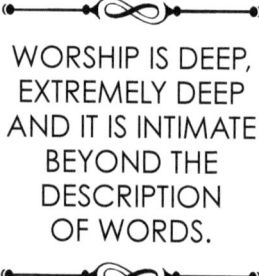

WORSHIP IS DEEP, EXTREMELY DEEP AND IT IS INTIMATE BEYOND THE DESCRIPTION OF WORDS.

I would share a few with you, note that after these encounters/visions, my spiritual life shot up to a level, I personally can't explain.

1.

I was worshiping and praying to God on the plane one day from Minnesota to Chicago. I had a vision and I saw myself in front of the throne of God. Jesus was sitting on a throne next to Him.

I was kneeling down with my hands lifted so high up, worshipping God with everything within me.

God was depositing 'things' into me. The more surrendered I was, the more He filled me up with something.

That something was His Spirit.

I heard the Holy Spirit telling me that God was equipping me, through His Spirit, with the necessary things I needed for the rest of the journey and for the things He was calling me to do in that season.

2.

I was praying and worshipping God and inviting the Holy Spirit into a building that I was in and I saw a powerful wind push out demons. The wind opened the door and the demons walked out.

3.

I stayed in my room and worshipped one day from 8:30pm to 12:00am. After I was done, I heard the Lord tell me that I had been shot up to a new level in my spiritual life. I literally saw myself being shot up so high into the skies.

These were encounters I had during my intimate worship sessions with the Lord. These encounters had me absolutely slain and changed by God!

To be intimate with the Lord, you need to be an intimate worshipper. You need to be able to throw all distractions away and run to the feet of Jesus. I live at His feet and I've told Jesus that right there is where I want to be forever. Trust me, down at the feet of Jesus is indeed the highest place to be – Humble yourself before God and He will lift you up. (James 4:10)

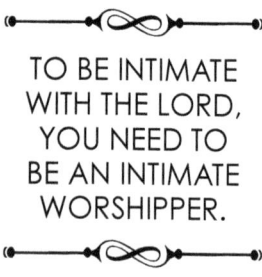

TO BE INTIMATE WITH THE LORD, YOU NEED TO BE AN INTIMATE WORSHIPPER.

How do you sustain an intimate worship life?

Stay in constant communication with God by interacting with the Holy Spirit always! Make sure your environment is conducive for God's presence. Always set the atmosphere. Personally, I make sure my environment is soaked and thick with God's presence. I do this by constantly playing worship music or sermons. Even if I have to step out of my room, I will leave the preaching on or keep the worship music playing. It charges the atmosphere in my room and that's exactly what I need to stay intimate with my Father. You are in control of both your physical and spiritual environment. God has given you that power spiritually, and physically, that's why He gives us wisdom. BE WISE and ensure that your environment is always conducive for the Holy Spirit to move!

CHAPTER 8

HOLD TIGHTLY TO THE WORD

"Every word of God has proven to be true. He is a shield to those who come to him for protection.'

Proverbs 30:5 AMP

"The law of the Lord is perfect; it gives new strength. The commands of the Lord are trustworthy, giving wisdom to those who lack it."

Psalm 19:7 GNT

"Faith is taking God at His WORD"

– Leonard Ravenhill

If you've lived long enough, you know that life is not easy. Struggles can hit you so hard that you'd rather wish you were never born but trust me

God's plan Is greater and more powerful than your problems.

As I type this, I am currently walking through an impossible situation. It feels as though I'm walking into the unknown. I have no idea what's next. I can't even guess how my help is coming neither do I know when my help is coming. But, there's one thing I know for sure and it's this: My Help cometh from the Lord.

GOD'S PLAN IS GREATER AND MORE POWERFUL THAN YOUR PROBLEMS.

...but there's one thing I know for sure and it's this: MY HELP COMETH FROM THE LORD.

And you know the beauty of all this? I actually don't need to know when my help is coming or how it is coming, all I need to know is that God is on my side and my help comes from HIM!

Sometimes, life hits you really hard and there isn't much you can do, sometimes there's absolutely nothing you can do and that's okay. All you need to do is to hold on to the WORD of God. Store it very deep in your heart. Purpose in your heart to believe and trust everything in God's WORD. It doesn't matter how impossible your situation may be, all you need to do is to cling tightly to the promises of God and never let it go.

The deeper you dive into God's WORD, the more intimate you get with Him. "In the beginning was the WORD and the WORD was with GOD and the WORD WAS GOD." John 1:1.

When you dive deeper into God's WORD, you go deeper into the mind and heart of God. Trust me, the more you know God, the more you fall in love with Him because God is flawless.

During specific seasons of my life, I take a verse and hold it very dear to my heart. I purpose in my heart and mind to believe the WORD and cling tightly to it. We have belittled and underestimated the power in God's WORD for far too long. God's WORD is so sure. It is alive and active.

"For the word of God is alive and powerful. It is sharper than the sharpest two-edged sword, cutting between soul and spirit, between joint and marrow. It exposes our innermost thoughts and desires." Hebrews 4:12 NLT

So, don't give up, rather hold on to God's WORDS and PROMISES, Hold it dear to your heart.

Choose to believe it and experience the supernatural peace and joy that comes with it.

CHAPTER 9

DYING TO SELF

"I have been crucified with Christ; it is no longer I who live, but Christ lives in me; and the life which I now live in the flesh I live by faith in the Son of God, who loved me and gave Himself for me."

Galatians 2:20 NKJV

"Most people are half saved. They bring their sins to the cross but never get to the cross."

– Leonard RavenHill

Dying to self – one of the most difficult but most effective and fulfilling things to do. One way to unlock the power that is made available through your intimacy with God is by dying to your flesh and selfish desires. But, the question is, how does one just die to the flesh? First of all, you die to your flesh by constantly being yielded to the Holy Spirit. Then the next question is how does one just yield to the Holy Spirit? You stay yielded to the Holy Spirit by living a prayerful life!

Let me take you back the garden of Gethsemane where Jesus was betrayed by Judas Iscariot. He left His disciples around the entrance and went deep into the garden to pray. When He came back, He was disappointed to find them sleeping. Now, here's the thing. Jesus wasn't just disappointed with the disciples because they fell asleep.

Pay attention to what He says:

"And He came to the disciples and found them sleeping, and said to Peter, "So, you men could not keep watch with me for one hour? Keep watching and praying that you may not enter into temptation; the spirit is willing, but the flesh is weak."

Matthew 26:40-41 NASB

Temptation will always come but your ability to withstand temptation is in how strong your spirit man is. So, when you pray a lot and spend hours in the WORD, you feed your spirit and your spirit man grows stronger and stronger!

However, the sad truth is that rather, we put in so much effort doing things pleasurable and profitable to the flesh only. When we do this, we neglect our spirit-man and we become so weak. This makes us prone to temptation. Don't forget that the Bible says that physical exercise profits little but spiritual exercise profits much.

"For "physical exercise has some value, but godliness is valuable in every way. It holds promise for the present life and for the life to come."

1 Timothy 4:8 NET

The more time you spend building up your spirit-man, the more yielded you become to the Holy Spirit, and the more sensitive you become to His still small voice.

Some of us are so dead in the Spirit that we need some divine CPR! But, there's always hope and good news when Jesus is involved. So here's your Hope – It's not a dead situation. And, the good news is this: It's never too late to try intimacy with God.

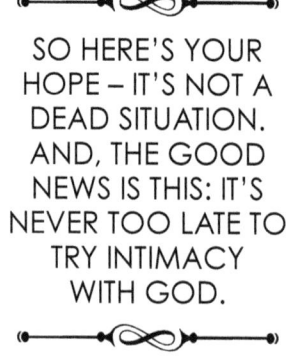

SO HERE'S YOUR HOPE – IT'S NOT A DEAD SITUATION. AND, THE GOOD NEWS IS THIS: IT'S NEVER TOO LATE TO TRY INTIMACY WITH GOD.

Personally, I always make sure my environment is conducive for God's presence. I make sure that my heart is not flooded with nonsense from the world. Our hearts and minds are flooded with so much nonsense that we find it so hard to see, hear or even feel God!

"For I determined to know nothing among you except Jesus Christ, and Him crucified."

1 Corinthians 2:2 NASB

It's an intentional decision to keep your eyes fixed on Jesus and the cross! Let that be you from today! Die to yourself, pick up your cross and follow Jesus!

CHAPTER 10

GOD, DO YOU TRUST ME?

> "Look! The cry of the people of Israel has reached me, and I have seen how harshly the Egyptians abuse them. Now go, for I am sending you to Pharaoh. You must lead my people Israel out of Egypt."
>
> Exodus 3:7-10 NLT

"God never uses anyone greatly until He tests them deeply." – A. W Tozer

Can God trust you to do His work? Can God trust you to deny yourself certain pleasures for the salvation of a lost soul? Can God trust you to pray and intercede on behalf of His people? Can He trust you to fast? Can God trust you to tarry long in His Presence? Can God trust you to deny yourself some sleep for the sake of others?

Many times, we wonder why God hasn't put us up on a platform but can He trust you with the unsaved people around you? You want God to take you to the nations to preach yet you won't serve in your local Church. Can God trust you at all?

Sometimes, it's just a person that God has placed in your life for godly mentorship and He wants to see how you treat that one person. Our God is that good shepherd that leaves the ninety-nine and attends to the one. Are you a good shepherd? We want God to take us to the nations, but we can't even help that one sheep to find its way back home. How can God trust you with precious souls?

I want you to take a pause and reflect. Reflect on your life. Reflect on the "little" opportunities God has given you to serve Him. That task you were given that you pushed to the side because you thought it was too "small." If God can't trust you with the little, how can He ever elevate you and how can He ever bless you with much?

No matter where you find yourself now, just know that there is a specific reason why you find yourself there at this time. Are you giving God your all? Are you giving God your best? Are you giving God a hundred percent?

Something very vital you will need as you pursue the work of the Kingdom wholeheartedly is this:

"And whatever you do, do it heartily, as to the Lord and not to men," Colossians 3:23 NKJV

Your service to God will be greatly tested and if you do it to please men, you will give up and miss out on a great blessing. Let God be your focal point as you serve Him. Make it literal – Whatever you do, do it as unto the Lord! Constantly keep your gaze fixed on Jesus as you serve Him, whether in Church, in a ministry, at home, or wherever. Let this be your motto: As unto the Lord and not man!

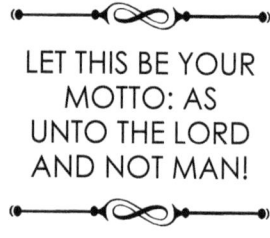
LET THIS BE YOUR MOTTO: AS UNTO THE LORD AND NOT MAN!

God doesn't just raise people up, He tests their faithfulness in that small ministry group and in that local Church. Be someone that God can trust and serve wholeheartedly wherever you find yourself.

Ask God, "God, do you trust me?" and ask Him to make you someone He can trust with a divine assignment.

CHAPTER 11

TO LIVE IS CHRIST, TO DIE IS GAIN!

"For to me, to live is Christ, and to die is gain." – Paul

"To me the only important thing about living is Christ. And even death would be profit for me. If I continue living in the body, I will be able to work for the Lord. But what should I choose—living or dying? I do not know. It is hard to choose between the two. I want to leave this life and be with Christ. That is much better."
Philippians 1:21-23 ICB

"Shadrach, Meshach, and Abednego answered and said to the king, "O Nebuchadnezzar, we have no need to answer you in this matter. If that is the case, our God whom we serve is able to deliver us from the burning fiery furnace, and He will deliver us from your hand, O king. But if not, let it be known to you, O king, that we do not serve your gods, nor will we worship the gold image which you have set up.""

                          Daniel 3:16-18 NKJV

Let me tell you the truth, as scary as it may sound, once you're living for Christ, even if you should die, you lose nothing. Rather, you gain the privilege of uniting with Christ. How beautiful it will be – Hugging Jesus and sitting at His feet. You get to talk about your struggles for the Kingdom as HE shows you His nail pierced hands, feet and sides. What a glorious moment!

Okay okay, come back here. You're still alive so there's WORK to be done! Once you're alive, Jesus should be your focus and motivation. Never let a day go by without carrying out your God-given assignment!

Having this – to live is Christ and to die is gain – as your life motto means that you're willing to boldly live for Christ. And, even when the persecutions come your way, it will give you even more reason to go all out for God!

Take a closer look at Shadrach Meshach and Abednego – they were instructed to bow down to an idol. Everyone did except them. The King gave them some more chances to bow down to the gold image but that wasn't it. There was a death penalty attached if they failed to comply with the rules. They were going to be thrown into a burning furnace with the heat turned up 7-times hotter than normal!

These three bold men still said NO! WE WILL NOT BOW DOWN TO YOUR god! But, here's the part that takes me out, they went on to say that "Our God will deliver us out of this fire BUT LET IT BE KNOWN TO YOU THAT EVEN IF HE DOESN'T, WE WILL STILL NOT BOW DOWN TO YOUR god!"

MY GOD!!!

The level of boldness here, my human brain can't comprehend! These guys understood that even if they had to die, they had ABSOLUTELY NOTHING to lose!

What about Stephen?

Stephen full of the Holy Spirit was going about preaching the truth! But as always some people did not like it. They basically wanted Him to shut up! But NO, NO, NO! Is there even something like that for a person on fire for the Lord?

Stephen was invited before the officials and he had the opportunity to shut up or "tweak" the Bible for the people to be happy but he did not! HE PREACHED THE TRUTH WITH BOLDNESS and these people were so angry that they stoned him to death. (Acts 7:54-60) Stephen preached his way into Heaven! Wow!

"The Jewish leaders were infuriated by Stephen's accusation, and they shook their fists at him in rage. But Stephen, full of the Holy Spirit, gazed steadily into heaven and saw the glory of God, and he saw Jesus standing in the place of honor at God's right hand. And he told them, "Look, I see the heavens opened and the Son of Man standing in the place of honor at God's right hand!" Then they put their hands over their ears and began shouting. They rushed at him and dragged him out of the city and began to stone him. His accusers took off their coats and laid them at the feet of a young man named Saul. As they stoned him, Stephen prayed, "Lord Jesus, receive my spirit." He fell to his knees, shouting, "Lord, don't charge them with this sin!" And with that, he died."

Acts of the Apostles 7:54-60 NLT

To live is Christ and to die is gain is not merely a metaphor, it's a lifestyle, let's live it out! There's work to be done!

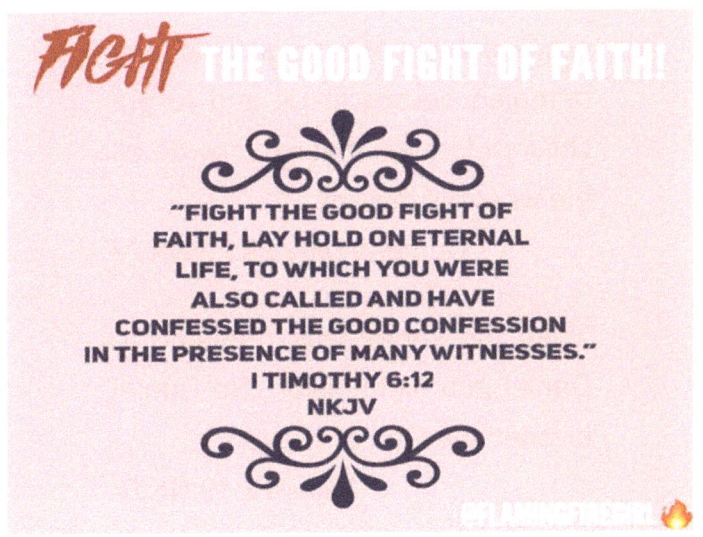

CHAPTER 12

THE SECRET.

"'The secret things belong to the Lord our God, but those things which are revealed belong to us and to our children forever, that we may do all the words of this law.'
Deuteronomy 29:29 NKJV

"Then the secret was revealed to Daniel in a night vision. So Daniel blessed the God of heaven."
Daniel 2:19 NKJV

It wasn't until I intentionally made it a point to spend hours in God's presence that I understood this secret. You see, before then, I was so desperate for God to open my eyes to see. I wanted to have encounters so bad. I wanted to see the angels, I wanted to dream all the powerful dreams,

The Secret.

I wanted to visit Heaven and all of the other cool stuff Church kids crave.

I never understood why I never saw or why I never heard but the sad truth was I wasn't spending quality time with God–praying for long hours and studying the Word diligently.

When Jesus and I became Besties and I would pray for long hours and communicate with the Holy Spirit throughout the day, the visions became many and the encounters, divine. I've had three different encounters with Jesus – two of which were actual encounters and the third a supernatural dream that shifted things in my life.

Yes, the secret things belong to God but He wishes to take you in on that journey of revealing more of Himself to you.

The same thing happened to Daniel, the King had a dream that no one could interpret. You could say it was a "secret" that only God knew at the time but it is definitely no coincidence that Daniel prayed and unlocked the secret of Heaven.

"Then Daniel went home and told his friends Hananiah, Mishael, and Azariah what had happened. He urged them to ask the God of heaven to show them his mercy by telling them the secret, so they would not be executed along with the other wise men of Babylon. That night the secret was revealed to Daniel in a vision. Then Daniel praised the God of heaven." Daniel 2:17-19 NLT

There's a huge difference between someone who prayed and someone who prays. Daniel didn't just pray that one time, Daniel was a man of prayer! That was Daniel's super power – His prayer life. Daniel prayed so much that His prayer life landed him into the Den of hungry lions but tell me, is there anything too hard for the God we serve?

Your boldness in your faith can sometimes land you in trouble or in the Den of hungry gossips and backbiters but there's nothing that Jehovah can't deliver you out off!

No one in their right senses reveals deep secrets to a person they do not trust or a person they barely know. We want God to reveal things to us but we are not building our relationship with Him; we are not working out our salvation.

You can unlock the secrets of Heaven by living life with Heaven in mind. Let's be heavenly minded for this world is not our own. You are here for a specific purpose and until you get intimate with the

The Secret.

God of your life, you will be living outside His will for the rest of your life.

We love Jeremiah 29:11, we love the comfort in knowing that God has plans for us. However, the unfortunate truth is that, without intimacy with God, you have detached yourself from this good plan of hope. If you can believe that God has good plans for your life, then you should understand that if you are not intimate with Him, you're not in alignment with that plan. That plan is IN God and there is absolutely no way you can access it without INTIMACY – getting deep into God.

The secret is this: your intimacy with Jesus is everything because everything you need is in your intimacy.

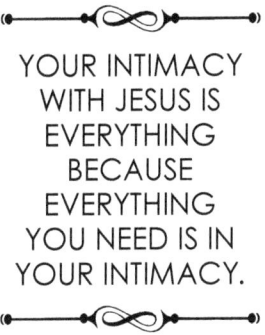
YOUR INTIMACY WITH JESUS IS EVERYTHING BECAUSE EVERYTHING YOU NEED IS IN YOUR INTIMACY.

Your purpose can never be discovered outside God. Shallow Christianity will never connect you to your purpose in life. It's only when you get deep with God that you discover who and what He created you to be.

"And such as do wickedly against the covenant shall he corrupt by flatteries: but the people that do know their God shall be strong, and do exploits."

Daniel 11:32 KJV

Know here means to interact with intimately. God created you to do exploits but without that INTIMATE relationship with Jesus, you will do NO exploits for the Kingdom and in this world.

Give God your whole heart, allow Him to consume you with His fire and watch the secrets of Heaven unfold before your eyes!

GET INTIMATE!

"LORD, I'M COMING!"

"MY HEART HAS HEARD YOU SAY, "COME AND TALK WITH ME." AND MY HEART RESPONDS "LORD, I AM COMING.""

PSALMS 27:8 NLT

It's about time!

www.ingramcontent.com/pod-product-compliance
Ingram Content Group UK Ltd.
Pitfield, Milton Keynes, MK11 3LW, UK
UKHW022119230426
12048UKWH00010BA/599